Introduc

The Cardigan Bay coastline still r
A Kittiwake guide to a long-distan...
of Cardigan to the stunning National Nature Reserve on the Dyfi estuary 60 miles away was published in 2000 and has proved very popular. The route passes through small villages and towns, each with their own unique character, and it is these villages that form the base for this second book on the Cardigan Bay Coast.

Fifteen circular walks, which range from 1 – 6 miles, have been selected, all starting and finishing on the coast. The choice demonstrates the wonderful variety of this coastline – you can walk along the gorge at Cilgerran; admire the views from the Iron-Age hill fort of Pen Dinas; explore ancient churches, or spend time watching bottlenose dolphins and seabirds close inshore.

Many of the walks are over land that is either owned by the *National Trust*, or is *Heritage Coast*, a *Site of Special Scientific Interest*, or a local nature reserve.

About the author:
Liz Allan was born in South Wales where she spent most of her childhood exploring the Gower coast through play. Having lived and worked in Australia and London, she now lives in New Quay in Ceredigion, and is the County's Coast and Countryside Project Officer. She also organises guided coastal walks on selected weekends throughout the year. Details at www.weekend-walking-wales.co.uk

Illustrations:
Lynne Denman, a practising artist and exhibition designer, working mostly in the field of local and natural history.

Cover photographs:
Penny Sharp, a local photographer specialising in land and seascapes.

WALK 1
CARDIGAN TO ST DOGMAELS

DESCRIPTION Cardigan is a lively little town on the lovely river Teifi. **Walks 1 & 2** both start on the south side of Cardigan bridge, this one going up river to the abbey remains at St. Dogmaels, and the other downstream to Cilgerran Castle and back along the spectacular gorge. Before setting off it is worth paying a visit to the town's Heritage Centre in the nearby 18th-century warehouse at Teifi Wharf, which is *open daily 10.00 – 17.00pm during the season.* The centre houses a permanent exhibition that traces the colourful history of the town from pre-Norman times, and is packed with interesting information. The walk is 3 – 4 miles long.
START Old Cardigan Bridge. SN177457.

1 Head south from the bridge and take the first right onto the St. Dogmaels road. On the left hand side look out for the bridleway signpost and follow this green lane as it climbs towards Parc Yr Eithin farm. *Coppiced hazel on the lane's banks provides welcome shade when the sun shines and shelter when the icy northerly winds blow in from the sea.* On reaching the farm, go through two bridlegates and over a stile and continue along a muddy track to the road. *Make sure to look across to your right as you navigate the muddy track in order to catch sight of the glorious view opening up of the mouth of the estuary and Poppit Sands.*

2 At the road, turn right and continue past bungalows until the road bends away to the right and begins its descent into St. Dogmaels. Here, and opposite the large house *Plas Newydd*, look to your left to see a track leading off sign-posted to the property Cefn Uchaf. Follow this bridle-way for just over half a mile, until it emerges at Blaenwaun Baptist Chapel *which was rebuilt in 1885.* Follow the road as it bears right around the end of the graveyard and continue downhill. *At the gates to the Chapel there is an old slate notice next to the slate and stone stile, with a none too welcoming message from one Mr. James warning visitors and chapel-goers to behave themselves when entering onto the premises or, one suspects, face the dire consequences! A little further down the road, past an extremely old red post box with intriguing decorative post-horns, there is a rather interesting brick baptism pool on the left.*

3 At the T-junction, turn left and immediately right at the footpath sign. Continue straight ahead along this lovely track that winds its way along the top of a wooded valley *with the occasional glimpse of the quarried rock faces far below.* This track will take you all the way into the village of St. Dogmaels.

4 Turn right where the track ends and continue until the T-junction where you turn right. Follow this road downhill into the village, pass the Mace shop on your left and look for a little lane on your right opposite Lion House (*with two stone lions conveniently placed on the gate pillars*). Turn right into this lane and continue to the church and Abbey. *St. Dogmaels' Abbey was founded about 1115 on the site of a monastic community of the old Welsh type, and a daughter house of the French Abbey of Tiron. The Sacramus Stone propped up inside against the back of the church dates from the 5th or early 6th-century.*

5 Leave the Abbey by the gate opposite the duck pond and turn right, following the road past the garage to the T-junction. Turn right and immediately left at the road to *Mwtshur.* Continue straight ahead down this road, pass an old green kissing gate on your left, and carry on towards Parc y Pratt which is clearly sign-posted. This next stretch of the path is well way-marked, crossing fields and a meadow with flag iris, meadow sweet and willow in a rather soggy corner. The

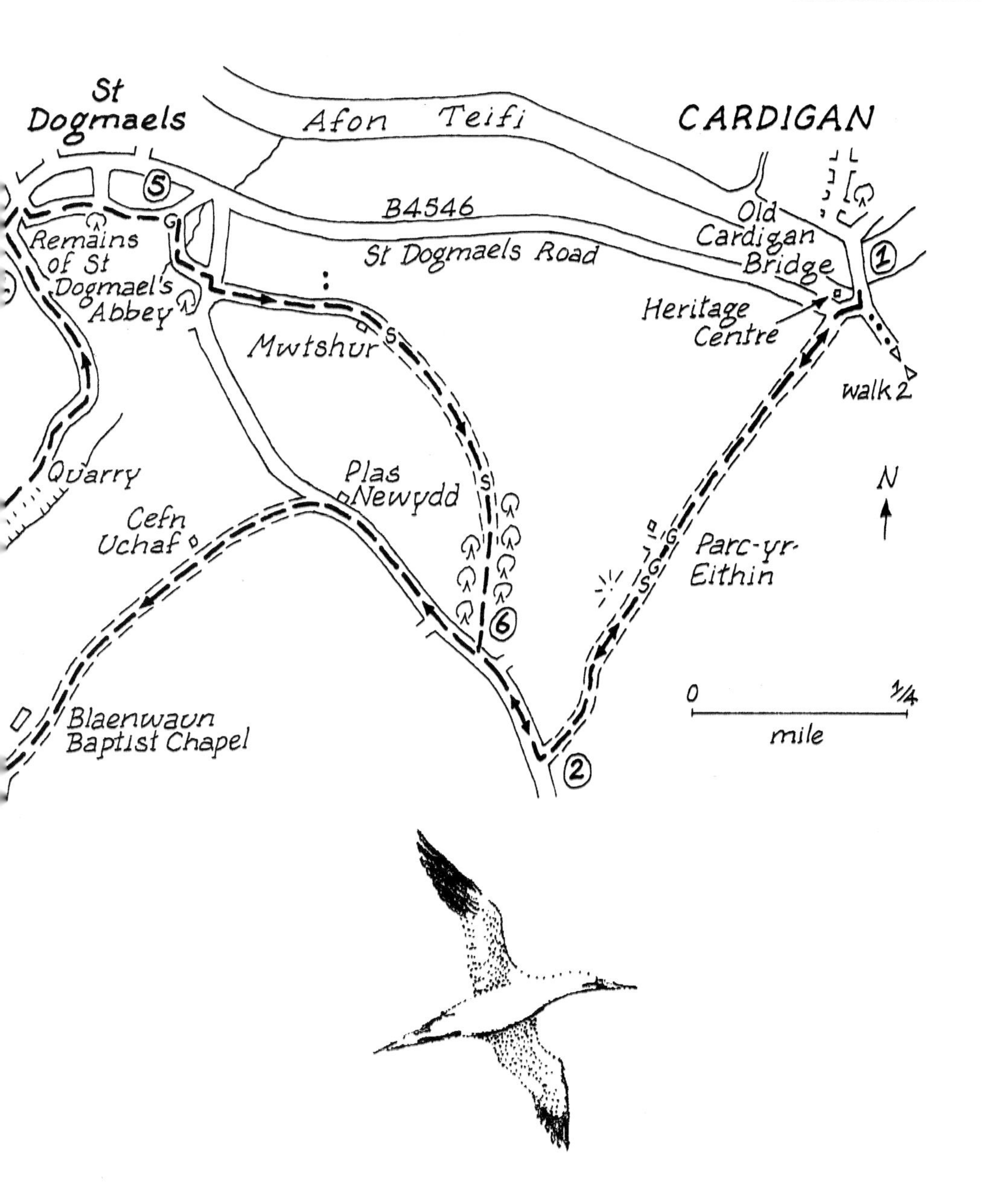

path bears right across the field just before it enters a small wood. Continue through the wood until it emerges back onto the road.

6 Turn left and follow the road back to the bridleway on the left that takes you once again past *Parc-yr-Eithin* farm and drops down into Cardigan and back to the river.

WALK 2

CARDIGAN TO CILGERRAN

DESCRIPTION This is an absolute corker of a walk, so it is well worth spending a day here if you can, as there is so much to see and explore both en route at the Welsh Wildlife Centre and on arrival at Cilgerran. As well as visiting the castle, the nearby Coracle Centre is of interest, and the guided canoe trips down the gorge are great fun. This walk is 5 miles long.

START Old Cardigan Bridge SN 177457

1 From Cardigan Bridge head south up the hill ignoring the first turning on the left, signposted Cattle Mart. Where the road bears to the right towards the roundabout, carry straight on along a residential street, marked as a no through road and continue walking for a few metres to the main A487. Cross this main road with care to the stile opposite.

2 A fieldgate and stile ahead on your right leads you onto a track down the hill into the Welsh Wildlife Centre. This track can get very wet and muddy, *but a boardwalk at the bottom of the hill makes the going a little easier as it takes you through a lovely expanse of bullrushes and onto the otter trail. These freshwater marshes began to develop after the railway line was built in 1885 along the banks of the Teifi river. The bird hide on the left is a good place to sit for a while and watch for herons or a hunting marsh harrier.* Continue along the boardwalk and path to where you emerge onto the tarmac drive that takes visiting cars to the Centre.

3 Turn left onto the drive and then immediately right up a track to the house. *Here you can feed the chickens if you have a spare 50p in your pocket*, otherwise go past the house and continue straight ahead along the track which now leads you into the woods. This track runs straight along the bottom of this lovely oak covered hillside for about 400 metres before bearing left up a path with a derelict cottage and white house on the right.

4 Turn right where the path emerges onto a farm access track. This track leads you down past some farm outbuildings to Cilgerran with the castle soon coming into view on your left. Take the first left where the track comes out onto a tarmac road. and then immediately right down some concrete steps to the bridge. Follow the track on the left up to the tarmac road and carry on straight ahead into Cilgerran village. The entrance to the castle soon comes into view on the left.

5 Leave Cilgerran along the same road you came in, and look for the footpath sign on the right about 200 metres from the castle entrance. This path descends down to a bridge and climbs up the other side to a tarmac road. Turn left, and after a few metres look in the bank on the right for an old stone stile next to a more modern wooden one.

6 Follow right hand edge of field to corner and stile. The path now enters a dense conifer plantation but is clearly way-marked, and crosses two wooden bridges. The dark conifers eventually give way to a deciduous woodland and the track continues along the top of the spectacular gorge with open fields on the left and the river flowing way below.

7 At the stile, turn immediately right onto a rather muddy lane and continue walking along the edge of the gorge. Where this lane emerges into an open field straight ahead, a stile on the right leads you back down into the woods and the river below. The path is now along the banks of the river and leads you to the *Wildlife Visitor Centre.*

8 Pass the Centre on your right, and follow the tarmac drive which takes you back to the entrance to the otter trail. Turn right and retrace your steps, along the boardwalk and through bullrushes, to Cardigan.

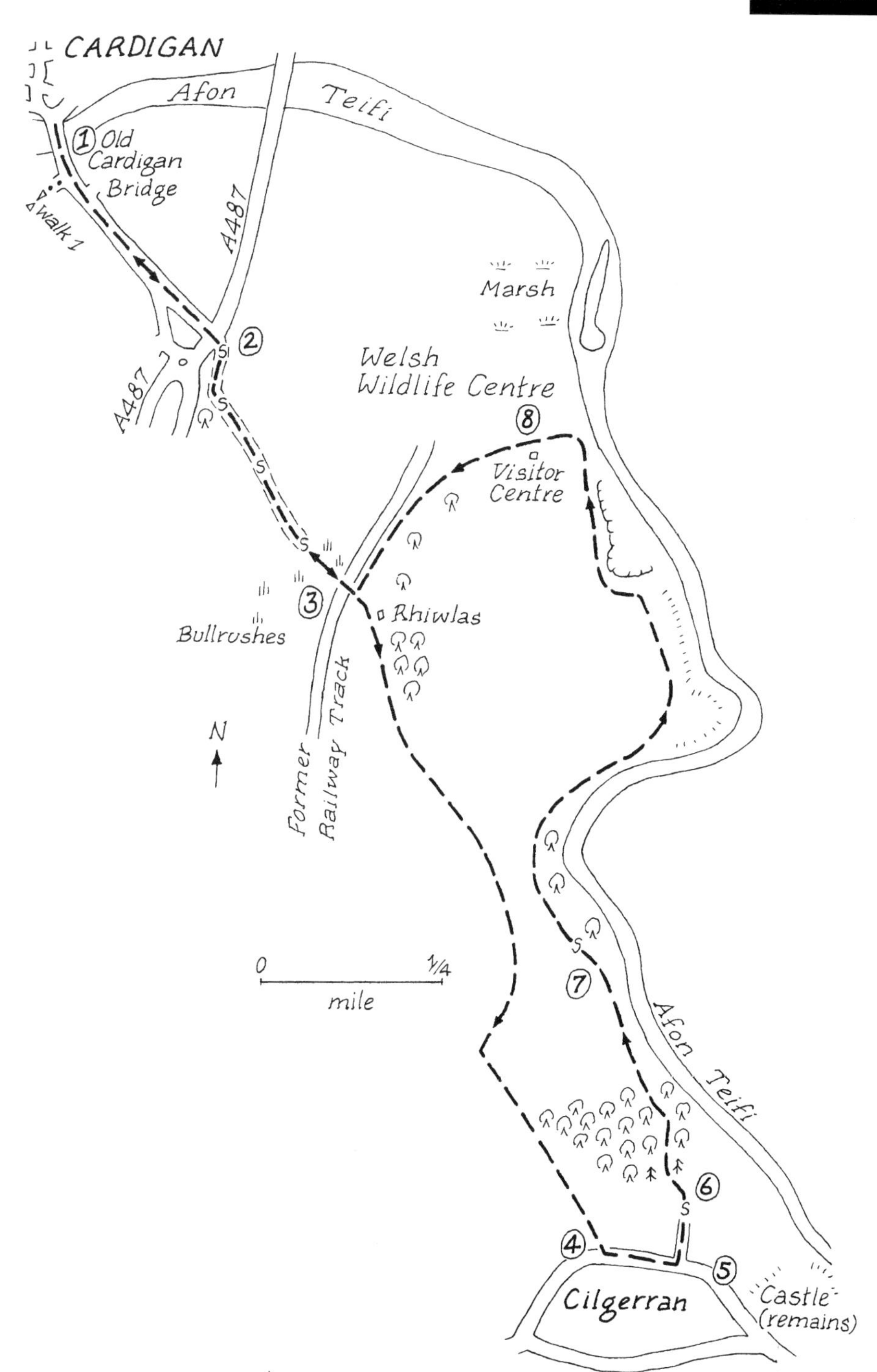
CARDIGAN
Afon Teifi
1 Old Cardigan Bridge
walk 1
A487
A487
2
S
S
S
S
Marsh
Welsh Wildlife Centre
8
Visitor Centre
3
Rhiwlas
Bullrushes
N
Former Railway Track
0
1/4
mile
7
S
Afon Teifi
6
S
4
5
Cilgerran
Castle (remains)

WALK 3

ST MICHAEL'S CHURCH, PENBRYN

DESCRIPTION: The area of Penbryn is a very ancient settlement indeed. St. Michael and all Angels is possibly the oldest church in Wales and the Pillar Stone found standing in a field between the church and Tresaith gives a clue as to the length of time people have settled around these parts. The Pillar Stone bears the Latin inscription: '*The body of Corbalengus lies here, an Ordovician*'. Corbalengus was thought to be a Celtic chieftain who died sometime during the period AD 120-160. Penbryn beach and surrounding area is now owned and managed by the National Trust. This walk is just one mile long (at most!).

START: Start from the delightful café (seasonal), just 1 mile along quiet country lanes from the A487 at Sarnau. Here you can fortify yourself with all sorts of treats before heading off. SN 290525.

This walk is ideal for those who only like the shortest of interludes between refreshment breaks ....

1 From the car park and café take the lane down to the beach. Turn left over the wooden bridge and the path starts to climb up the other side of the valley. Where the path forks, take the steps on the right and continue climbing up the hill.

2 The path now emerges onto the top of the cliffs to give fine views down on to the beach. *Ahead, the Aberporth headland, with its missile testing range, can be seen.* The path swings back to the left to enter the woodland once more. *Dense ferns carpet the woodland floor.*

3 At the finger-post, turn right towards the church. Through the kissing-gate, the church looms overhead on the right. Way-markers point the direction across the field to the gate where you emerge onto the tarmacked road. Turn right and continue for a few metres before arriving at the church.

4 On leaving the church, retrace your steps to the finger-post down the hill, where you now turn right in the direction of the car-park. Steps lead you down the steep bank to the river and wooden bridge. The steps on the other side take you straight back to the car-park.

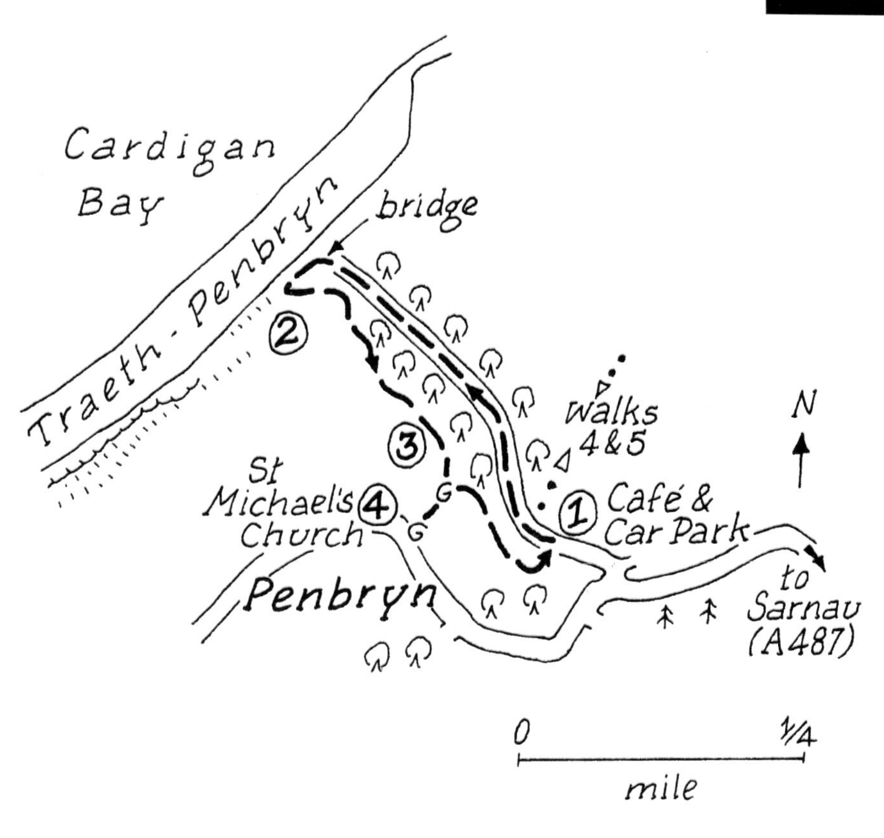
Cardigan Bay
Traeth - Penbryn
bridge
2
3
St Michael's Church
4
G
G
Walks 4 & 5
N
1
Café & Car Park
Penbryn
to Sarnau (A487)
0
1/4
mile

WALK 4

PENBRYN TO CAPEL MORFA

DESCRIPTION: This is a gentle circular walk through interesting woodland, quiet farm lanes and along open coastal path.
START Start from the delightful café (seasonal), just 1 mile of quiet country lanes from the A487 at Sarnau. SN 290525. This walk is 2 miles long.

1 Leave the café and take the sign-posted track to the left of the farm buildings. Through the field-gate, you begin a gentle ascent up an ancient track-way which cuts through a gorse, heather and bracken covered slope. The sound of stonechats perched on the gorse accompanies you.

2 Turn right at the footpath sign-post to Capel Penmorfa and continue through a gate and past the lovely old house of Troed-y-rhiw which has been owned by the same family for four generations. Ignore a track with a rather ancient tractor in the middle of it and continue downwards until a grassy track branches off to the left. The grassy track now leads you along a lovely wooded slope with the sound of a gurgling stream a little way below. *Some fine old beech trees marked by generations of local children with their initials provide some welcome shade.* Resist the temptation to wander off the path to visit the horses in the meadows on your right, but carry on until the chapel of Pen Morfa comes into view.

3 Climb over the old stone stile to the right of the capel and turn left onto the road. Continue past the capel and take the first left, sign-posted '*Morfa Isaf Farm B&B*'. Continue along this farm lane and go straight ahead at the junction sign-posted *Morfa Isaf.* Passing the farm buildings a footpath sign-post points to the right through a field-gate.

4 Follow the track as it stretches down towards the sea. The path now meets up with the coast-path which will take you all the way to Llangranog if you turn right. Turn left, and you start to head back to Penbryn. The coast-path now starts to descend towards Traeth Bach (little beach), but then climbs once again steeply without ever reaching this lovely small sandy cove. Once over the stile at the top of the slope, the path continues uphill over fields until reaching again the top of the ancient track which you took at the start of your walk. Turn right onto the track and begin your descent back to the café and that welcome cup of tea.

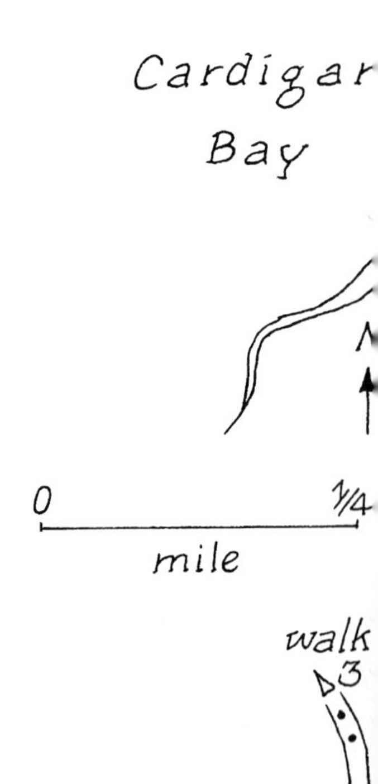

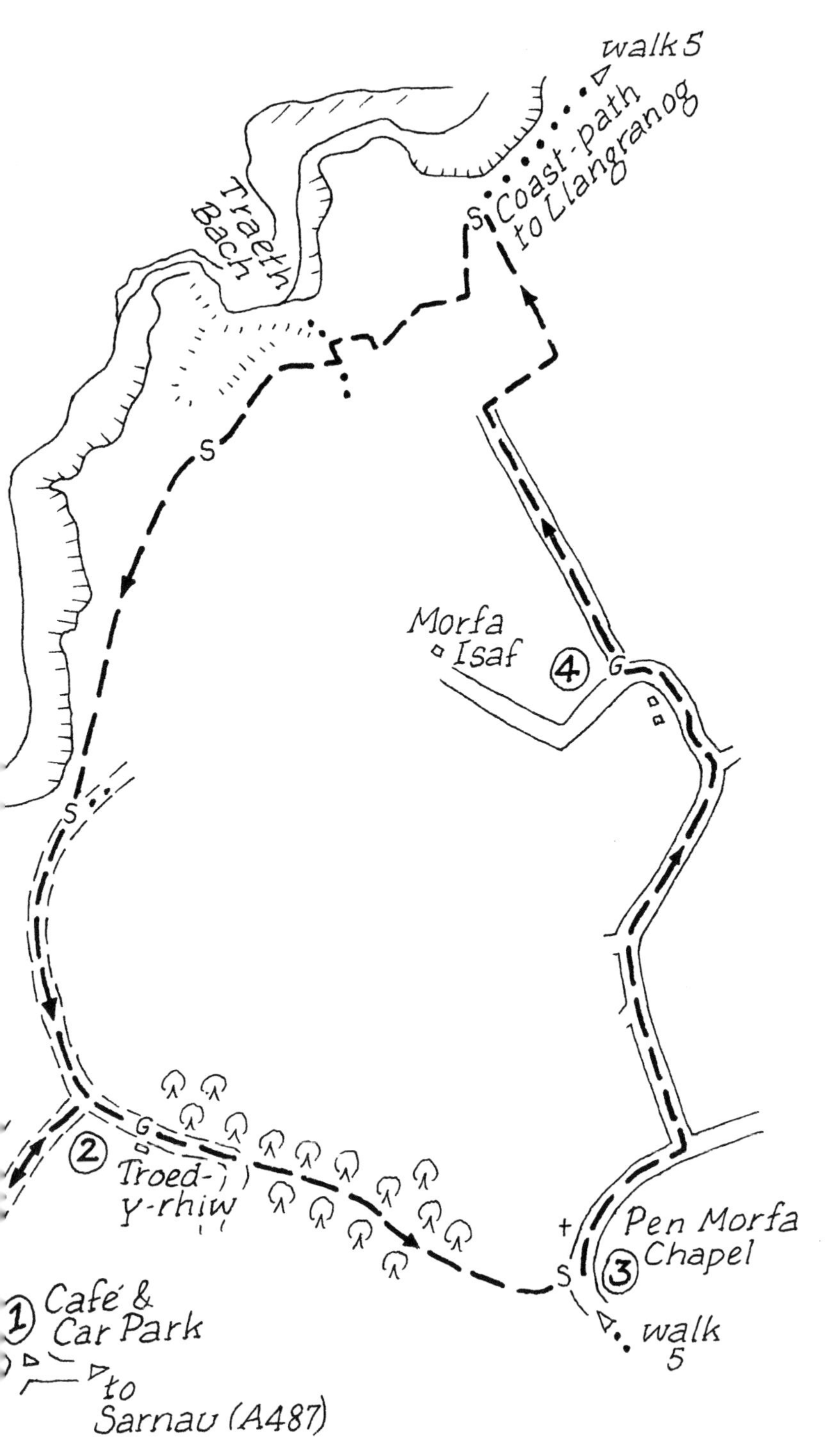
walk 5
Coast-path to Llangranog
S
Traeth Bach
S
Morfa Isaf
4
G
S
G
2
Troed-y-rhiw
Pen Morfa Chapel
3
S
walk 5
1
Café & Car Park
to Sarnau (A487)

WALK 5

PENBRYN TO LLANGRANOG

DESCRIPTION: This is the longest route from Penbryn. This lovely walk follows the coast-path to Llangranog and then sweeps back along pretty wooded valleys and lanes. Length about 6 miles.
START: The Llanborth car park at Penbryn. SN 290525.

1 From the Llanborth car park at Penbryn, the footpath is sign-posted at the left of the farm. Through field-gates, an ancient track-way climbs the gorse, heather and bracken covered hill *and gives fine views of the sweep of Penbryn beach and the coast beyond.*

2 A stile on the left at the top of the climb leads away from the track, and the path now crosses fields and descends to pass close to a small sandy cove, before climbing steeply once more to the cliff tops. This path is well sign-posted and easily followed all the way to the little village of Llangranog.

3 Leave Llangranog by the road that twists up the hill from the side of one of the village's pubs, *The Pentre Arms.* As you climb, ignore the road that twists off to the left, and continue climbing until the road ends at the bungalow '*Morwelin*'. The path continues straight ahead along an track to an old iron kissing gate that leads into a field.

4 Cross the field, keeping more to the left, and then along a muddy track on the edge of a wooded, scrub hill-bank. Where this track ends, look to the left to see a rough path climbing up the bank. After a few metres scramble, bear right until the path emerges into a field. Look ahead and the farm buildings can be clearly seen. Head for the field-gate through which the path emerges onto a farm track. Turn right along the track and bear left through field gate that takes you past *Eiddfa Farm* on your right. Follow this track until it emerges onto the road where you turn right. Continue along this quiet road for about 350 metres, passing a number of properties on both sides.

5 At the footpath sign turn left along a track that will lead you down into the lovely wooded Hoffnant valley. Where the track begins to descend, look for the track leading off to the left and continue along this until you reach the road. Turn right, and follow this road until reaching the T-junction.

6 Turn right and the road starts to climb towards the chapel Pen Morfa. Climb the slate stile on the left just before the chapel, and bear left across the field to pick up the path that continues through the woods to emerge onto the track leading to the property *Troed-y-rhiw.* Pass this lovely old house on your left and continue along the track which leads you back out to the coast-path, and the descent back to the Llanborth car-park.

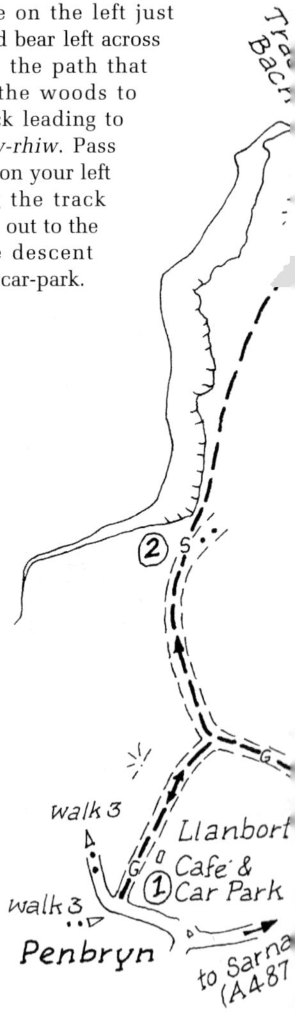

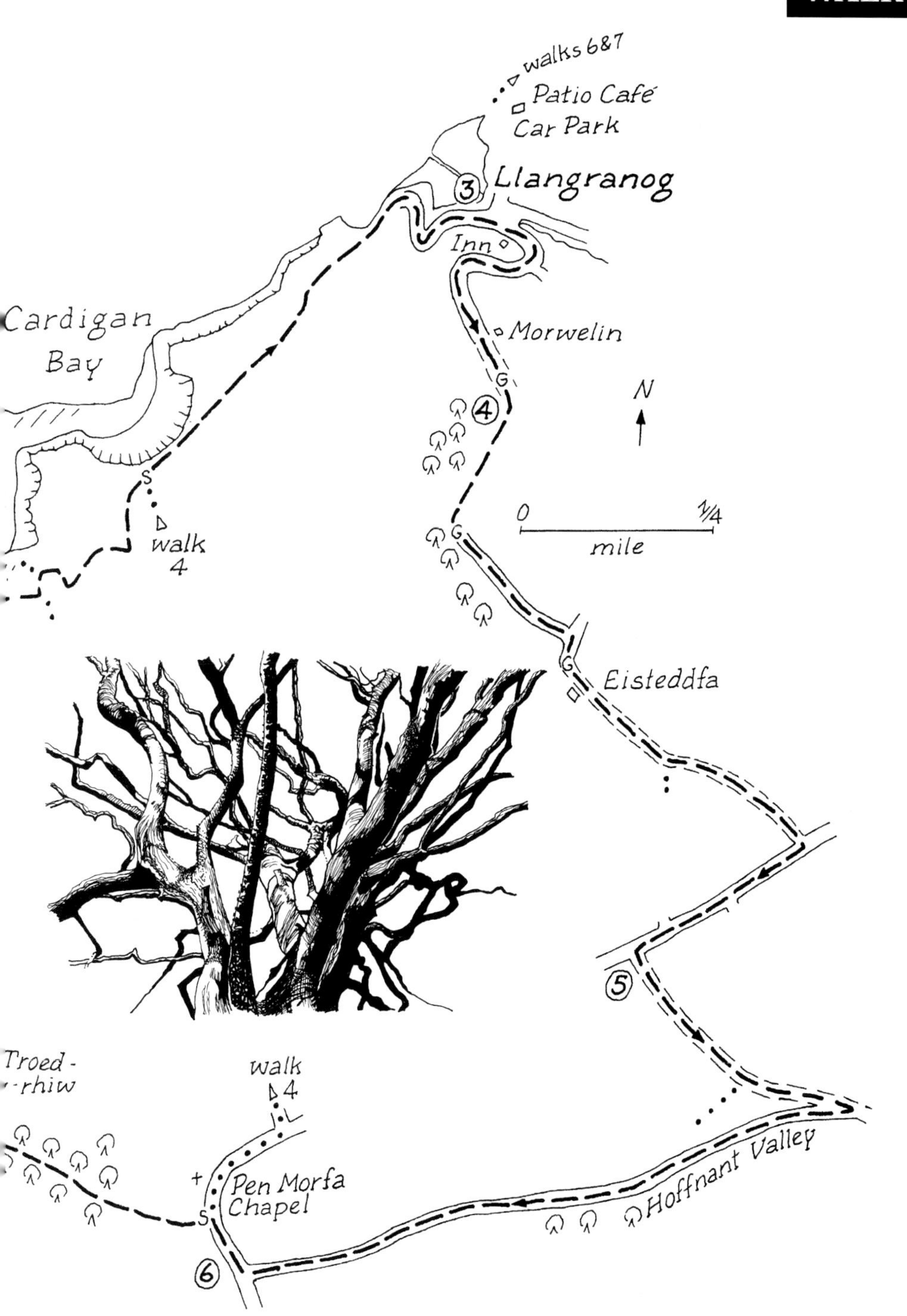
walks 6&7
Patio Café
Car Park
Llangranog
3
Inn
Cardigan
Bay
Morwelin
G
4
N
S
walk
4
G
0
1/4
mile
G
Eisteddfa
5
Troed-
-rhiw
walk
4
Pen Morfa
Chapel
S
Hoffnant Valley
6

WALK 6

YNYS LOCHTYN AND PEN Y BADELL HILL FORT

DESCRIPTION: It is difficult to imagine large wooden ships being built on Llangranog's small beach in the 1800s. A glimpse of another aspect of the area's colourful maritime history can be seen on the mural on the wall of the 17th century Ship Inn. The painting of The Ship is named after Black Bart, said to be the most successful pirate of all time. This walk is 2 miles long.

START: Llangranog beach SN316538. B4321 from A487 at Brynhoffnant (2 miles); B4334 from Pentregat (3½ miles). Bus service available from Cardigan.

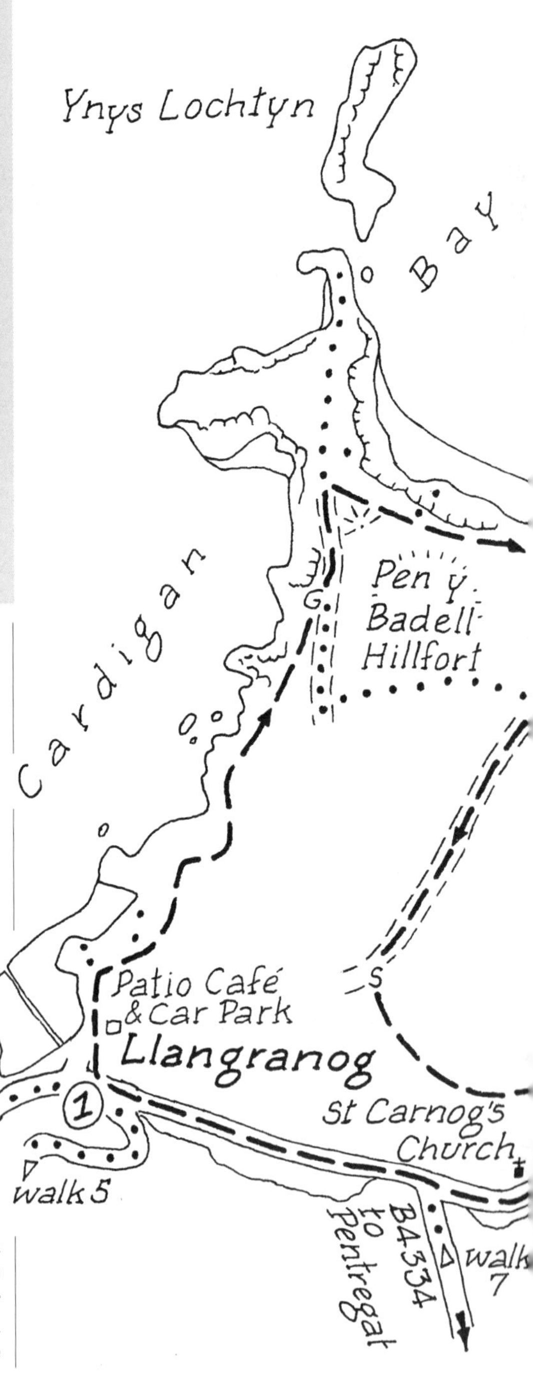

1 Take the steps leaving the northern edge of the beach, past the Patio café. The coastal path climbs towards Pen y Badell, an imposing Celtic hill fort. When you reach the gate directly in front of you, turn left along the track and circumnavigate the hill fort *which is covered in purple heather and yellow gorse during summer. Listen for the sounds of chough, a blackbird like bird with red legs and beak, or the screech of the peregrine overhead. Looking down at the promontory, the small island of Ynys Lochtyn lies beneath you. This is a good place to watch for harbour porpoise and bottlenose dolphins feeding, or grey seals popping their heads above the waves.*

2 The path continues around the side of the hill, before climbing steeply. As you climb, keep bearing right, to join a tarmac track at the back of the hill fort. This track leads back down the hill towards a gate. Long before reaching this gate, turn left over a stile. Bear left as you climb once more across a rough pasture. The path leads inland across gorse

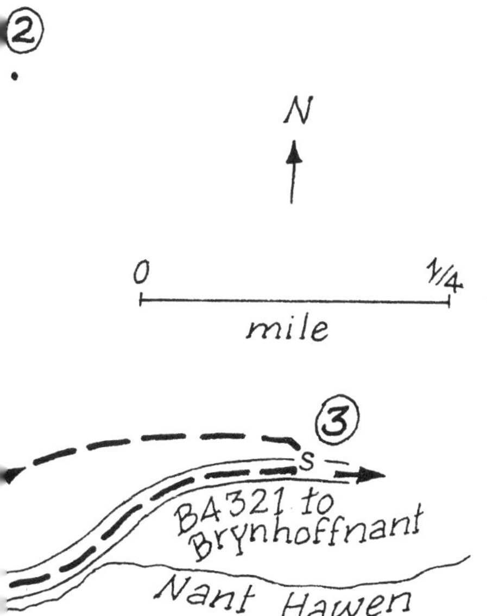

covered slopes along the top of the valley which leads out to the sea at Llangranog. *There has been a lot of gorse clearance along this path recently to protect the habitat of the pearl-bordered fritillary that is now an extremely rare butterfly in Ceredigion. These butterflies love to feed on the common dog violet and like sunny open areas with sufficient shelter nearby.*

3 The path emerges onto the approach road to Llangranog. Turn right, and continue back down towards the village. *Take time to visit the lovely St Carnog's church as you go, if you can bear to pass under the inscription over the door: 'Watch ye and pray lest ye enter into temptation'. In the churchyard, the gravestone of Sarah Rees, known as Cranogwen, is worthy of note. It can be found to the left of the church at the top of the bank next to the brown marble 'funnel' gravestone. Cranogwen was a remarkable woman of the 19th century, as she was a master mariner and taught generations of local boys in the art of deep sea navigation until her death in 1916.*

WALK 7
PIGEONSFORD VIA YNYS LOCHTYN

DESCRIPTION: This walk combines the dramatic openness at the promontory at Ynys Lochtyn with the shaded stillness of the woods at Pigeonsford. About 3 miles long.
START: Llangranog beach SN316538. B4321 from A487 at Brynhoffnant (2 miles); B4334 from Pentregat (3½ miles). Bus service available from Cardigan.

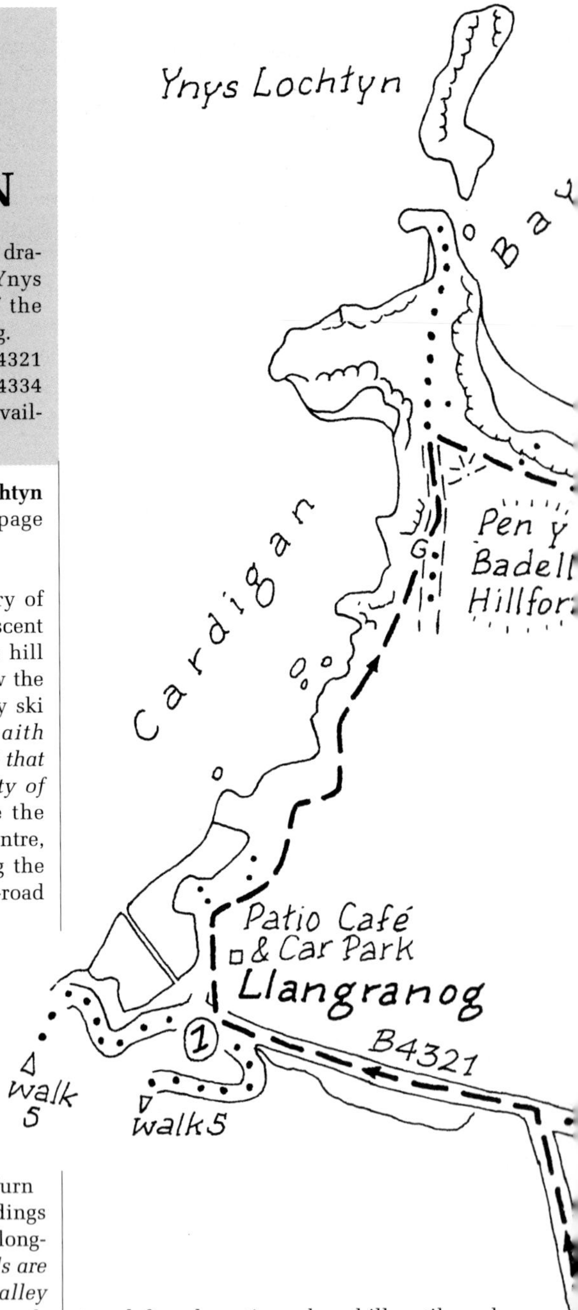

1 Follow instruction **1** of the **Ynys Lochtyn and Pen y Badell Hill Fort** walk (page 12).

2 As you leave the spectacular scenery of Ynys Lochtyn below and begin the ascent of the path on the northern side of the hill fort, bear left to continue north to follow the cliff top to the Urdd Centre with its dry ski slope. *This is one of two Urdd Gobaith Cymru centres (Welsh Youth Movement) that offers over 15,000 youngsters a variety of activities throughout the year.* Leave the coast now, and descend towards the Centre, where the route continues down along the Urdd access road until it reaches a cross-road with the B4321.

3 Cross over this road and continue straight ahead. *Just beyond the bridge, a sign invites you into the walled gardens at Pigeonsford. These are well worth a visit.*

4 Continue past the walled gardens until you see a footpath sign pointing to the right at Pigeonsford farm. Turn right along the track towards the buildings and the path continues straight ahead alongside the left of the property. *These woods are a delight and cover one side of the valley leading back down towards the sea.* The path through the woods emerges onto the road, where you turn right and continue down towards the B4321 again. At the T-junction, turn left and continue downhill until reaching a small lane leading off to the left. Take this little lane, and it takes you right back into the centre of the village.

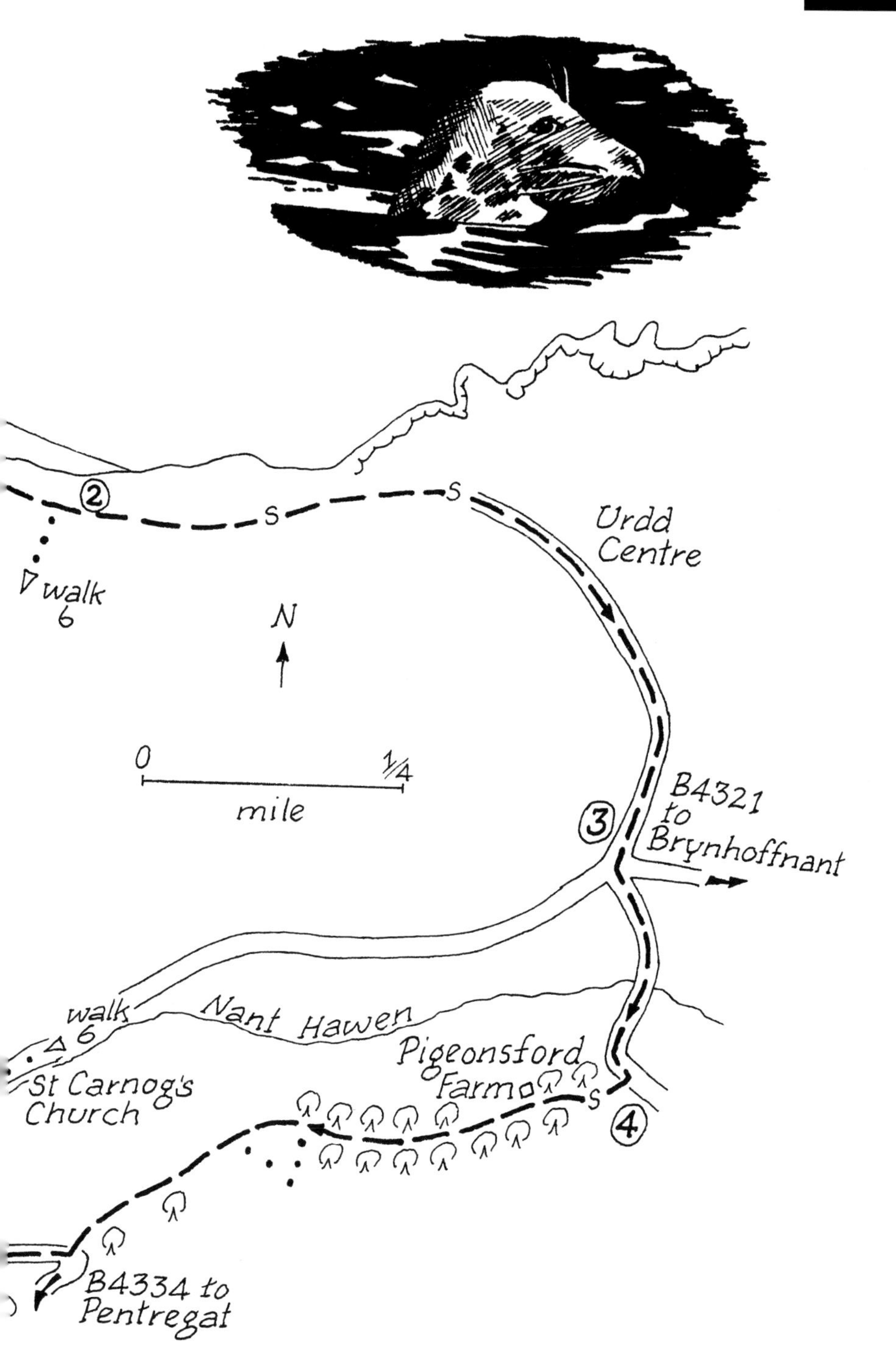
2
S
S
Urdd
Centre
walk
6
N
0
1/4
mile
3
B4321
to
Brynhoffnant
walk
6
Nant Hawen
Pigeonsford
Farm
S
4
St Carnog's
Church
B4334 to
Pentregat

WALK 8

CWMTUDU

DESCRIPTION: The little hamlet of Cwmtudu has something of a smuggling past. The little cove and surrounding dark caves were ideal for ships to arrive at the dead of night with their cargoes of salt and brandy. Ships would also arrive with limestone from South Wales which was brought ashore to be burnt in the old lime-kiln set back from the beach. Farmers from the surrounding lands would arrive by horse and cart and collect the lime to spread on their fields as fertiliser. This walk follows the coast-path to the iron-age settlement at Castell Bach, (little Castle), descends into a lovely cwm (wooded valley) and passes a 13th century church. About 2 – 3 miles long.

START: Cwmtudu beach. SN 355575. Country lanes from A487 to Llwyndafydd.

1 The coast-path starts at the kissing gate and snakes its way up the hill to reach level ground *and terrific views of Castell Bach below, and Birds Rock at New Quay in the far distance. Looking to the right, the roofs of Pen-y-graig farm can be seen.* Follow the path that leads to the farm and turn left at the farm buildings along a track.

2 After about a 100 metres, a finger-post points to the left and the direction of New Quay. At the kissing-gate, turn left down the hill, keeping to the left-hand side of the field alongside the old hawthorn bent over by the strength of the winds coming from the sea. Continue through a field-gate along the track that leads down the hill to a bridge over the stream. The finger-post points straight ahead up the wooden steps to the church. *The 13th century church of St. Tysilio, Llandysiliogogo was rebuilt in 1825, but is on the site of a Bronze Age ceremonial ground. St. Tysilio was an early Welsh saint*

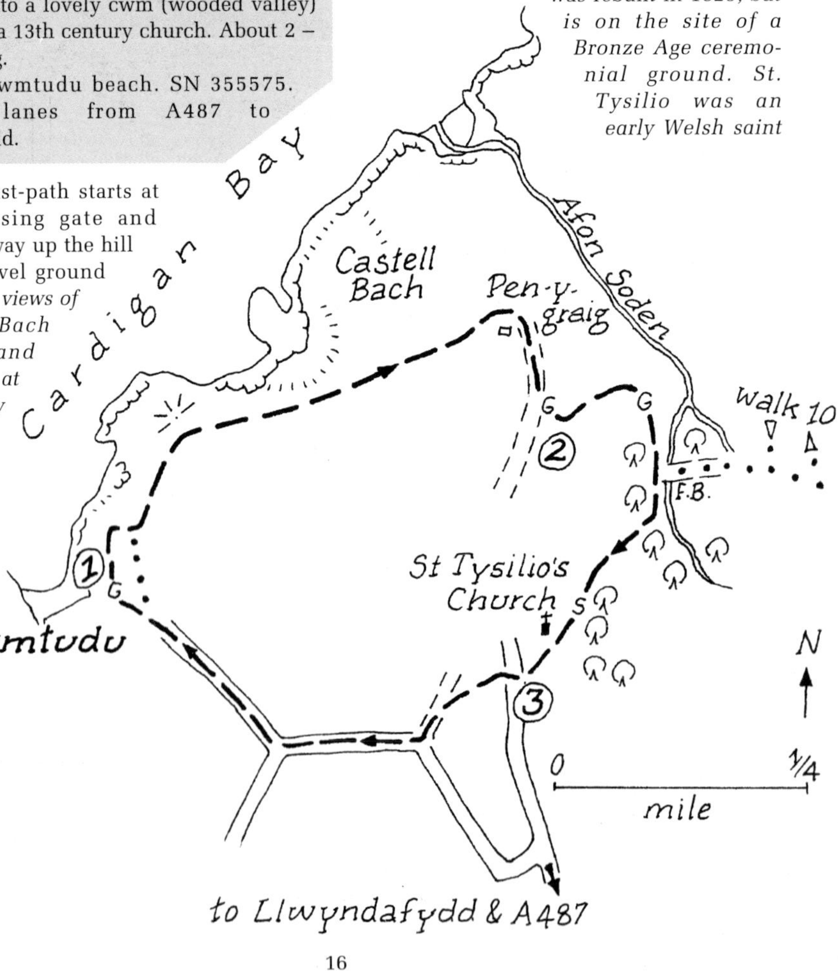

of the 7th century, but there is an ancient stone-lined spring to the north of the church that may be medieval in origin.

3 On leaving the churchyard, which was once more rounded than it is today, turn right and then left at the footpath sign at the kissing gate. Keep to the right of the field and at the next kissing gate, turn left onto the track that leads onto the road. Turn right onto the road that leads directly down the hill back into Cwmtudu.

WALK 9

NEW QUAY TO BIRDS ROCK

DESCRIPTION: The small fishing village of New Quay has become a popular destination for those wishing to get a closer look at Cardigan Bay's bottlenose dolphins. The bay is one of only two areas in Britain where there are resident populations of these animals, and the dolphins are often seen just off the end of the harbour. A patient vigil from the cliff tops can be rewarded with spectacular sightings of these marine mammals leaping clear out of the water. This walk is 2½ miles long.

START: End of Lewis Terrace. SN 385608. A486 from A487 at Synod Inn. B4324 from Llanarth. Buses from Aberystwyth and Cardigan.

This delightful short walk is a favourite of mine, and one that I can walk straight from home. During Spring and Summer the thousands of nesting seabirds perched precariously on the high cliffs are a visual treat.

1 Leave New Quay by the coastal path that starts at the end of Lewis Terrace (the top terrace of three rows of brightly painted houses above the fish processing factory at Target Rock). Brace yourself now as there is a steep haul up the path to the top. *Fortunately, the dolphins are often seen off Target Rock so there should be plenty of excuses to stop and stare out to sea in wonder, whilst catching your breath. At the top there are the remains of the old coastguard lookout – another good spot to admire the views.* The path to Birds Rock or Craig yr Adar is now very straight forward and takes you over some interesting sub-maritime heath. *The old field boundary walls are a picture with huge clumps of thrift or sea pinks, and sea campion. In May before the bracken has had a chance to take a hold, bluebells carpet the slopes as they lean down towards the sea. The rock formations of the sea-cliffs, which date back to the Ordovician age some 450 million years ago, begin to give you a clue as to what lies ahead. The alternating sand and mudstones layers of the ledges have become twisted and contorted overtime and now provide an ideal habitat for a wide variety of breeding seabirds.*

2 The path narrows to pass close to the cliff edge just after passing the National Trust's Craig yr Adar sign (there is an alternative path on the left for those suffering with vertigo). The path emerges into a small quarried area with Birds Rock far below you. *On warm, sunny days, this is a good area for butterflies if you can manage to resist the temptation to look down over the cliffs.*
Birds Rock is one of Wales' top ten seabird breeding colonies and is a spectacle in Spring with nearly 3000 guillemots perched precariously on the ledges of these ancient rocks. The cries from razorbills, kittiwakes, fulmar, cormorants and shags all contribute to the cacophony of sound audible above the crashing of the waves below. This is also an excellent spot for watching Atlantic grey seals that haul out on rocks between feeding trips, and give birth to their pups from August onwards in the more secluded caves and coves.
It is difficult to drag yourself away from this heavenly spot, but the most spectacular view awaits you from the coastguard lookout on the brow of the hill. This lookout was first occupied in 1924 and it is easy to see why this spot was chosen. Looking south, Cardigan Island, with the lights of the lighthouse at Strumble Head, can sometimes be seen, and towards the north the whole of the North Wales coastline and mountains come into view.

3 Leave the coastpath through the kissing gate opposite the lookout. Follow the track through the farm and out to a small lane.

4 Turn left and continue along the lane until reaching the Penrhiwlan pub on the road leading down into New Quay. Turn left, and continue downhill back into the village.

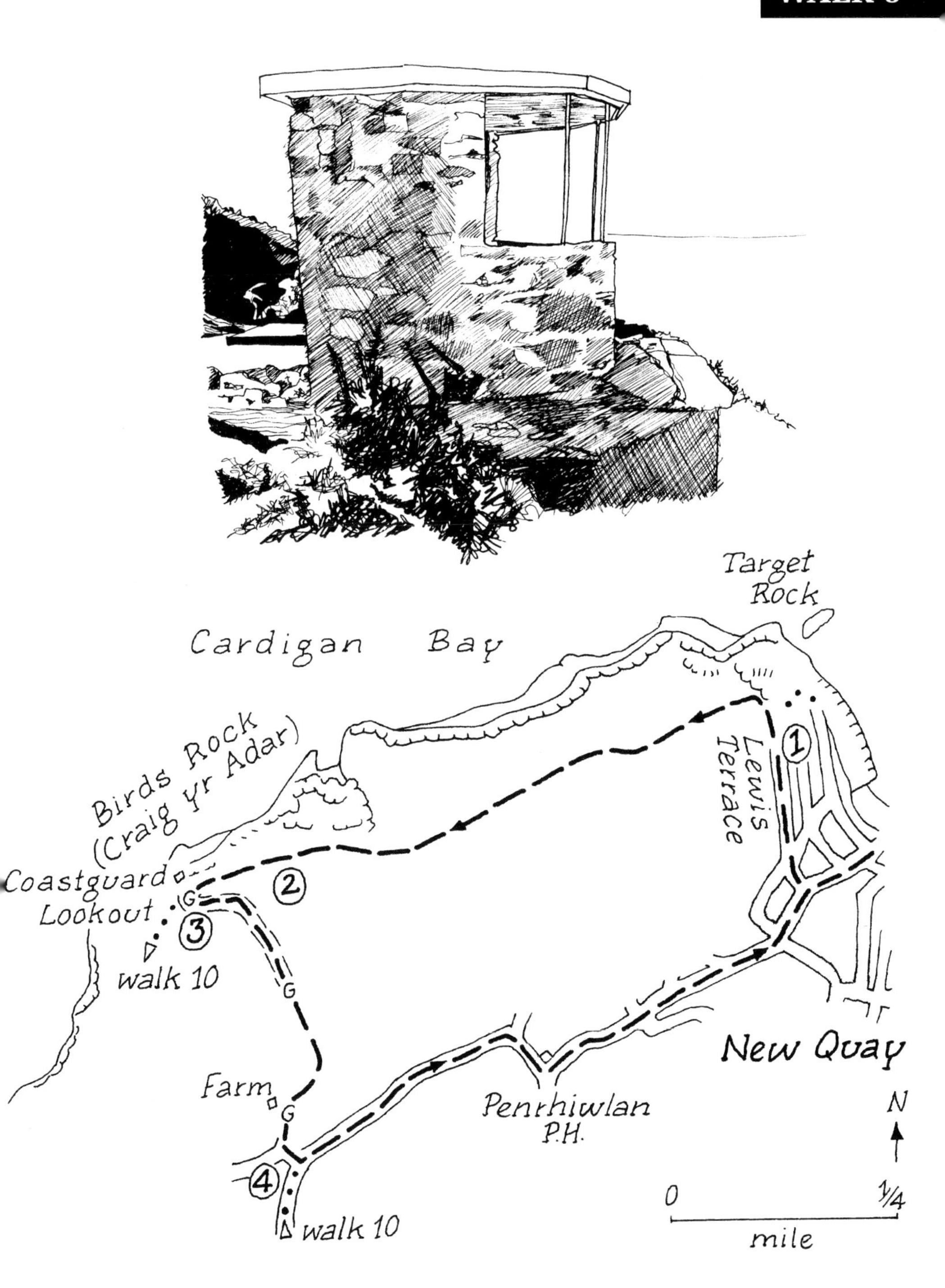
Target Rock
Cardigan Bay
Birds Rock (Craig yr Adar)
Coastguard Lookout
Lewis Terrace
1
2
3
4
G
walk 10
Farm
Penrhiwlan P.H.
New Quay
N
0
1/4
mile

WALK 10
NEW QUAY TO BYRLIP

DESCRIPTION: This walk follows the same route along the coast-path to the coastguard lookout at Birds Rock described in the New Quay to Birds Rock walk. It can also be joined up with the Cwmtudy walk at Cwm Soden for a longer circular. About 5 miles.
START: End of Lewis Terrace. SN 385608. A486 from A487 at Synod Inn. B4324 from Llanarth. Buses from Aberystwyth and Cardigan.

1 Follow instruction **1** and **2** for **Walk 9**. Pass the Lookout and continue along the coast-path. The path descends over fields, crosses a bridge and climbs steps to reach a finger-post pointing in the direction of Cwmtudy. Turn right here, and continue to descend down through the sheltered blackthorn slopes of Coybal. *A path leads away on the right to the quiet rocky beach.* Follow the path straight ahead (it can be very muddy), cross the stile and turn right. Look for the gap in between the windblown hawthorn trees on the right, and follow the path towards the bridge. The path then climbs steeply to reach the kissing-gate at the top of the hill. Go through this kissing-gate and follow the path to the lovely little cove at Cwm Soden.

2 The path now heads inland. *This has to be one of the most delightful coastal wooded valleys in the County. It is a treat to walk whatever the season. The cries of young buzzards circling overhead, and chiffchaffs welcoming the arrival of Spring, accompany you. Soon the sound of the cascading mini-waterfalls and rock-pools can be heard. A large meadow clearing on the right provides a diversion from the path to Byrlip but is worth it, as it leads down to the falls surrounded by carpets of wood anenome and snowdrops.* Coming back to the path, continue until reaching the National Trust sign '*Byrlip*' and finger-post which points back along the route you have just come. The longer route to Cwmtudu continues here. Bear right at this sign, cross two bridges and turn to page 16 for details of how to join the Cwmtudu circular walk as it leads off to the left up the steps to the 13th century church of St. Tysilio, Llandysiliogogo.

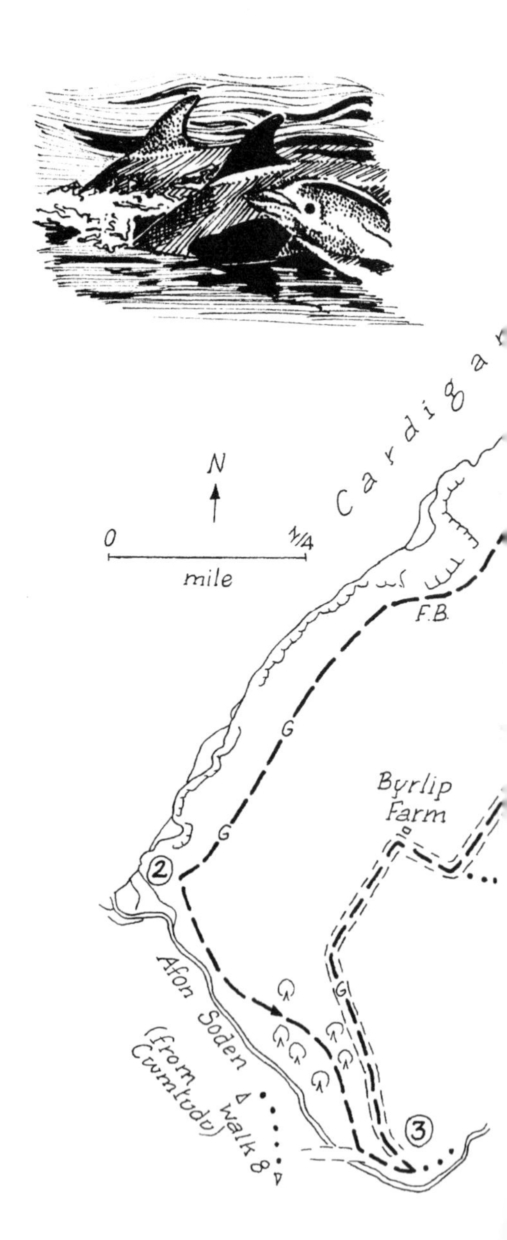

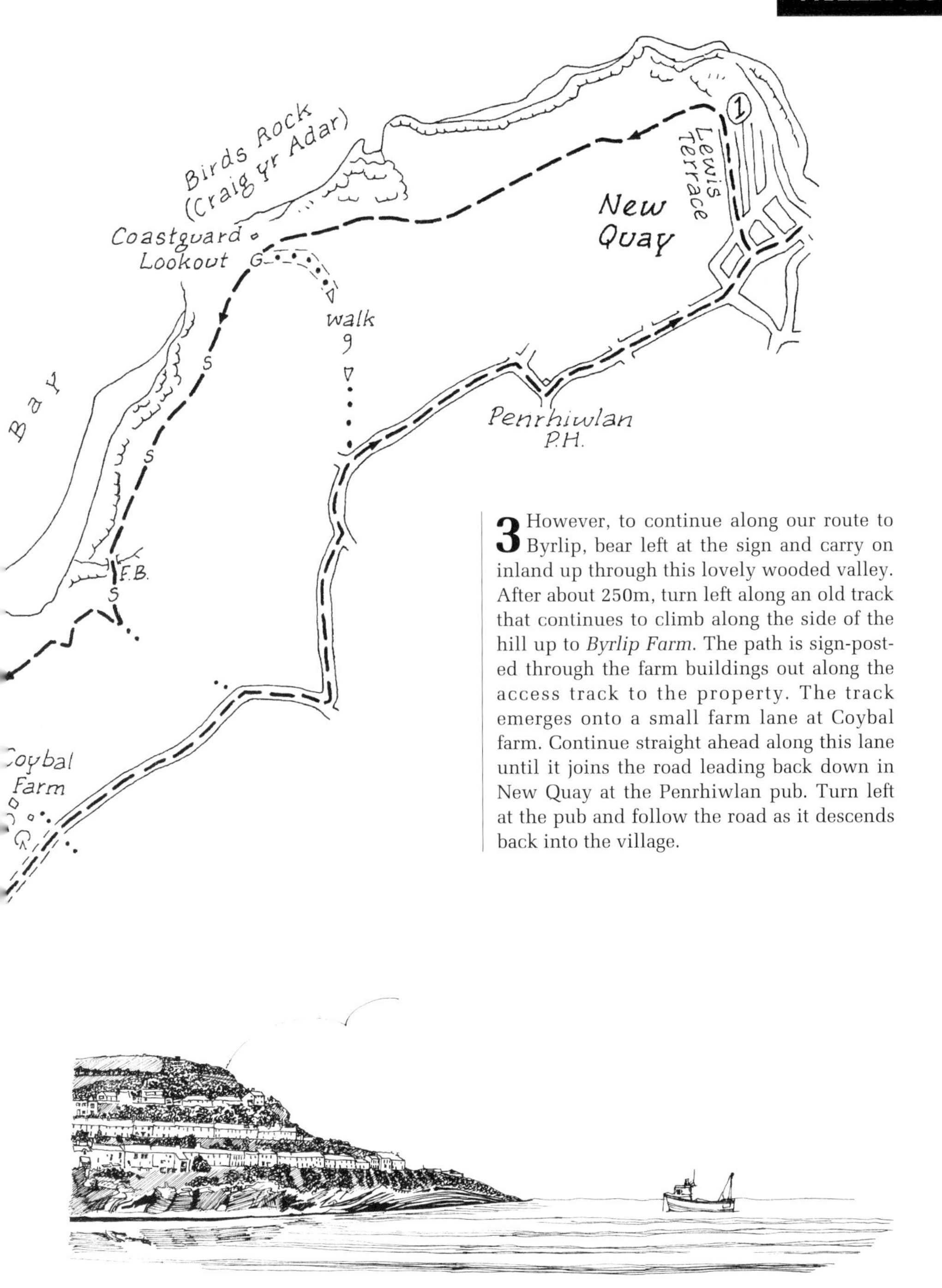

3 However, to continue along our route to Byrlip, bear left at the sign and carry on inland up through this lovely wooded valley. After about 250m, turn left along an old track that continues to climb along the side of the hill up to *Byrlip Farm*. The path is sign-posted through the farm buildings out along the access track to the property. The track emerges onto a small farm lane at Coybal farm. Continue straight ahead along this lane until it joins the road leading back down in New Quay at the Penrhiwlan pub. Turn left at the pub and follow the road as it descends back into the village.

WALK 11

ABERAERON TO ABERARTH

DESCRIPTION: This pretty town was created by the landowner, the Reverend Alban Thomas Jones Gwynne in the first half of the 19th century. The new Harbour Act meant that a new well-dredged harbour with stone piers and quaysides could be built, together with the elegant architecture of the residential streets. The railway line to Lampeter opened in 1911, but was not to last long. The walk to the old mansion and farm at Llanerchaeron follows the old railway line that closed in 1963. About 4 miles.

START: The road bridge over the River Aeron on the A487. SN 453628. Bus service from Cardigan, Aberystwyth, Lampeter.

1 The tarmac path follows the Aeron river upstream through Panteg woods. With the river rushing over the weirs on your left, this is a pleasant gentle start to both walks. Where the path meets the A482 road to Lampeter, turn left and cross the bridge. Turn right at the lane Bro-allt-y-graig.

2 For the route to Aberarth, take the first left at the lane Ffordd y Goitre. Check the tides before you leave, as the return leg of the walk is along the beach from Aberarth. This lane passes behind school buildings and climbs steadily up the hill. Just past a sign-post that warns HGV drivers of the unsuitability of their having ventured up this far, the path is found on the left. An old track leads uphill and as you climb steadily the sounds of energetic schoolchildren at play begin to fade in the valley below.

3 The path emerges from the shade of over-hanging branches onto a farm access track. Continue straight ahead along this access track, and follow the next signpost at a field-gate and stile. Once over this stile, however, ignore the stile on the left in the field, and continue straight ahead, keeping to the left edge of the field. The path over the fields is well sign-posted, so you can relax and enjoy the great views ahead and down to the coast. Soon, Aberarth and St. David's church come into view. The path begins to descend towards the church and emerges onto the road.

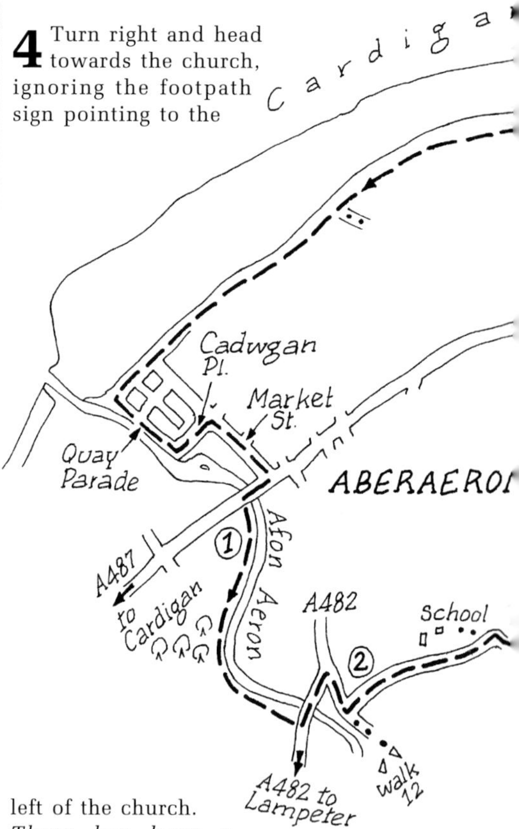

4 Turn right and head towards the church, ignoring the footpath sign pointing to the left of the church. *There has been a church on this spot since 900 AD. Vikings have raided on more than one occasion. The churchyard is worth spending some time in for its maritime interest.* From the church-yard, the path continues its descent towards Aberarth, *one of the earliest settlements along the Ceredigion coast.* Keep the line of the old harbour in sight, and head down towards the last stone cottage on the left edge of the village. Here you will find a stile and kissing-gate leading you down to the A487.

5 Turn right at the road and, TAKING GREAT CARE, cross over and take the

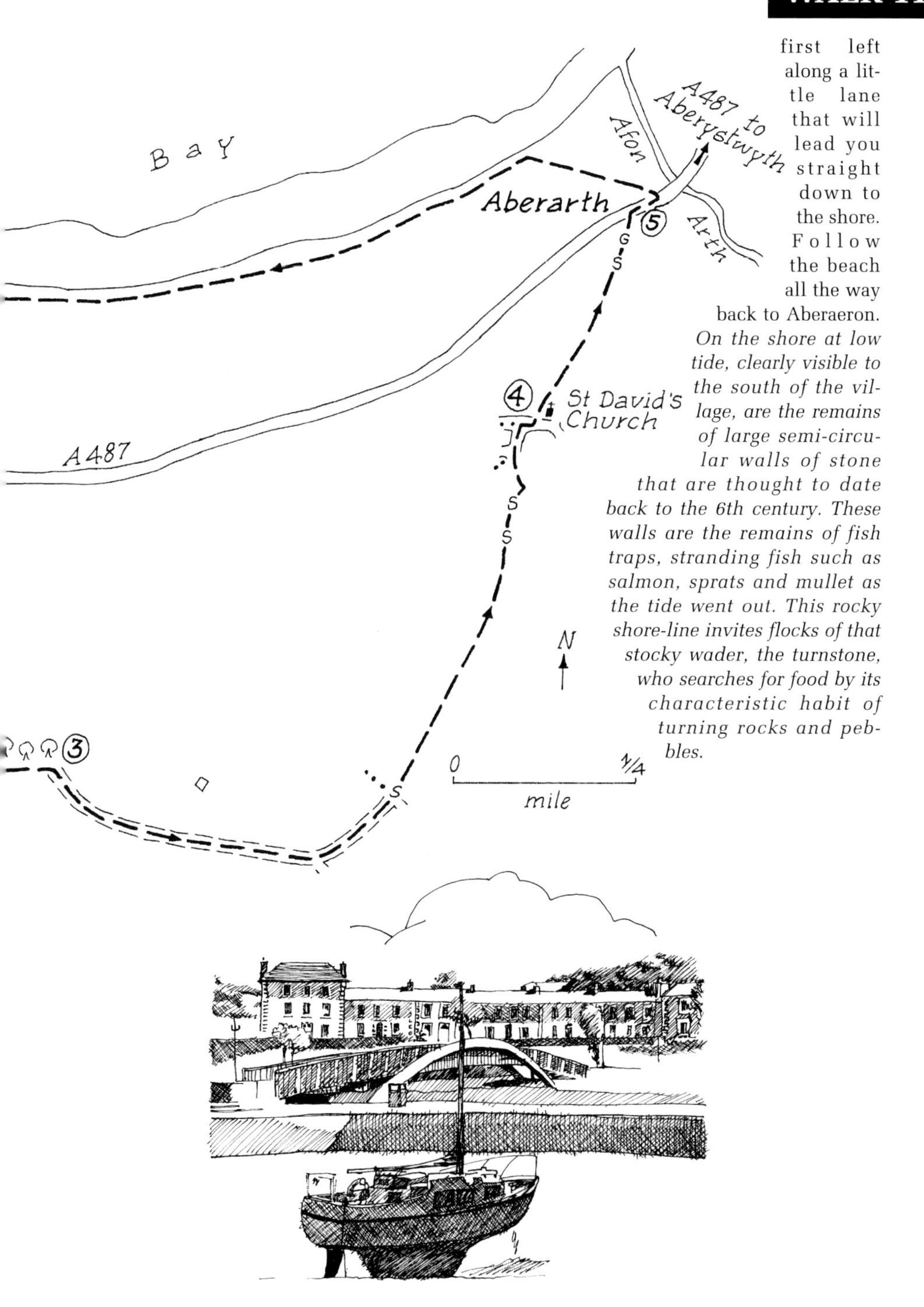

first left along a little lane that will lead you straight down to the shore. Follow the beach all the way back to Aberaeron. *On the shore at low tide, clearly visible to the south of the village, are the remains of large semi-circular walls of stone that are thought to date back to the 6th century. These walls are the remains of fish traps, stranding fish such as salmon, sprats and mullet as the tide went out. This rocky shore-line invites flocks of that stocky wader, the turnstone, who searches for food by its characteristic habit of turning rocks and pebbles.*

WALK 12
THE LLANERCHAERON ESTATE

DESCRIPTION: This walk follows the Aeron river upstream to the National Trust property at Llanerchaeron, a rare survivor of the core of a Welsh gentry estate. Guided tours around the farm buildings, walled garden and grounds are available *during June to September.* Check times and dates at the Tourist Information Centre in Aberaeron before setting off. About 3 miles.

START: The road bridge over the River Aeron on the A487. SN 453628. Bus service from Cardigan, Aberystwyth, Lampeter.

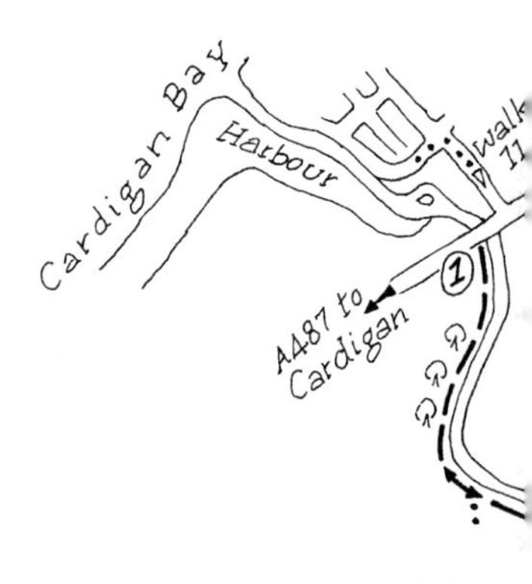

1 Follow instruction **1** for **Walk 11**. From the road bridge, follow the tarmac path through Panteg woods to where it emerges onto the A482. Turn left, and first right at Bro-allt-y-graig. Follow this lane until you reach a sign-post on the left leading you into the woods at Allt-y-graig. *The local town council have recently undertaken various woodland management tasks, and have created new paths through these woods.* Keep to the lower path that leads straight ahead, and bear right just after passing an old quarried area down some wooden steps that lead you back onto the lane. Turn left and continue along the lane past the '*No Through*' sign and the property *College Farm*. A finger-post guides you straight ahead along a path that leads down through the woods towards the old railway line.

2 Where the path and old railway line converge, cross over the stile straight ahead and continue along an old track that leads away to the left. This track leads to a derelict property and continues through the woods before emerging at a field. Cross over the field towards an opening diagonally opposite and continue along this field boundary to where the path emerges onto a farm access track. Turn left and immediately right, and the track continues through woods to a bridge that crosses the river Aeron. Over the bridge, cross the field towards St. Non's church *and the graveyard of Aberaeron's master mariners. One headstone tells the sad, ironic tale of one Gunner David Jenkins who, having survived four long, hard years in France during the First World War, was accidentally killed near Lampeter when he returned in 1919.*

Llanerchaeron Estate is now owned by the National Trust who have been restoring the John Nash designed house, built in 1795, and various farm buildings over the last 10 years or so.

2 A finger-post on the right just before the iron gates to the house leads over the field towards a bridge over the river. Turn left over the bridge and then immediately right onto the old railway track. This track now leads all the way to the Commins. Where the track emerges into a little parking area carry straight ahead and then turn left onto the lane which takes you back into Aberaeron.

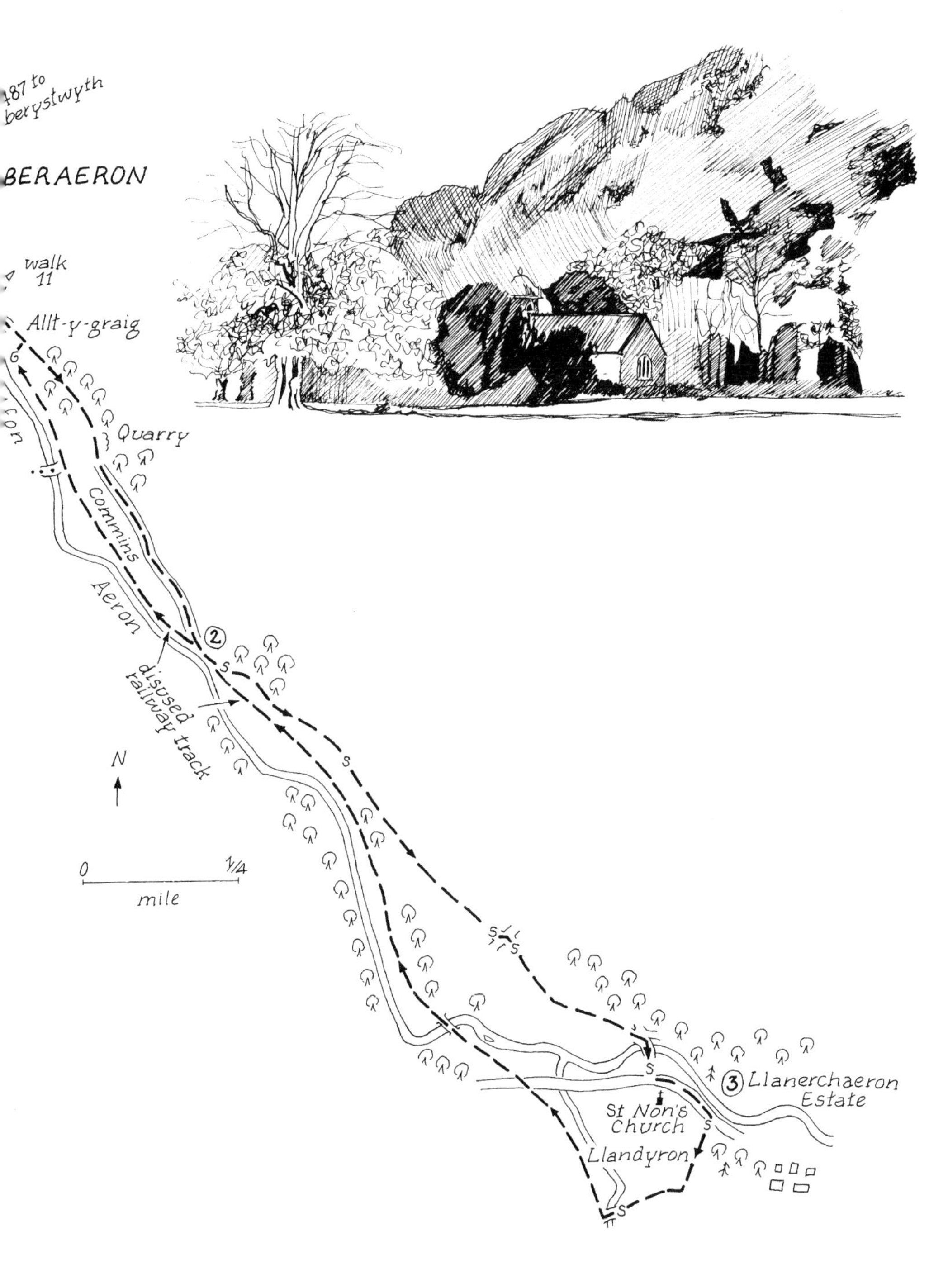
487 to
berystwyth
BERAERON
walk
11
Allt-y-graig
Quarry
Commins
Aeron
2
disused
railway track
N
0
1/4
mile
3 Llanerchaeron
Estate
St Non's
Church
Llandyron

WALK 13
HENFYNYW CHURCH

DESCRIPTION: Henfynyw is celebrated as the place where St. David spent his early years. This walk follows the coastal path south of Aberaeron before heading inland to the church, and the old lane that leads back down to the town. About 4 miles long.
START: The Tourist Information Centre at the end of the harbour in Aberaeron. SN 453628.

1 Turn left on leaving the Tourist Information Centre and head for the wooden bridge that crosses the river. Over the bridge the path bears right and continues along the tarmac road on the other side of the harbour. Pass the car-park and continue along the road as it runs parallel to South Beach. The coastal path starts at the end of this little road and begins its gentle climb out of Aberaeron, *passing the rather curious, Portmeirion-like, architecture of the pink house on the left.* The coastal path is well defined so ignore the little paths that come in from the left, particularly after crossing the wooden bridge. At the stream at Cwm Cilfforch, take care crossing as there is no bridge. *I walked this route in November 2000 after all that rain, and it was a bit tricky, but the time before that it had been OK. The ladder steps just after this stream should be approached with care also, as there has been quite a bit of erosion along this stretch in recent times.* At the next stile near Gilfach yr-halen, the way-marker points to the left up the hill. Once on the brow of the hill, the stile is visible in the right-hand corner of the field.

2 Turn left over the stile onto the *Cilcert Farm* lane. Continue along this lane until the field-gate at the farm. Look down the left-hand bank at this gate, and the stile and way-marker is clearly visible. Keep to the right-hand edge of this field for a few metres until you reach another stile. The path is clearly way-marked across the field with the farm outbuildings on your right to another stile which leads into a leafy old green lane. Go left at the next stile into a field and cross over towards the woods and stream. A stile leads you down to the bridge, and the path continues up the opposite bank to a field behind the church and house. The path skirts the edge of this field and emerges onto the A487 with the church on the right.

3 Cross over the A487 and continue straight ahead along the little road with bungalows. Turn left at the next turning and continue on this road until you reach a stile on the left just beyond some new farm buildings. Cross this stile and continue along the field edge until you reach another stile that leads onto an old track. This lovely little track drops down towards Aberaeron and gives fine views of the coastline and harbour. The track emerges onto a road opposite the *Clos Pengarreg Craft Centre.* A finger-post leads the way down towards the river and the stroll back into the town.

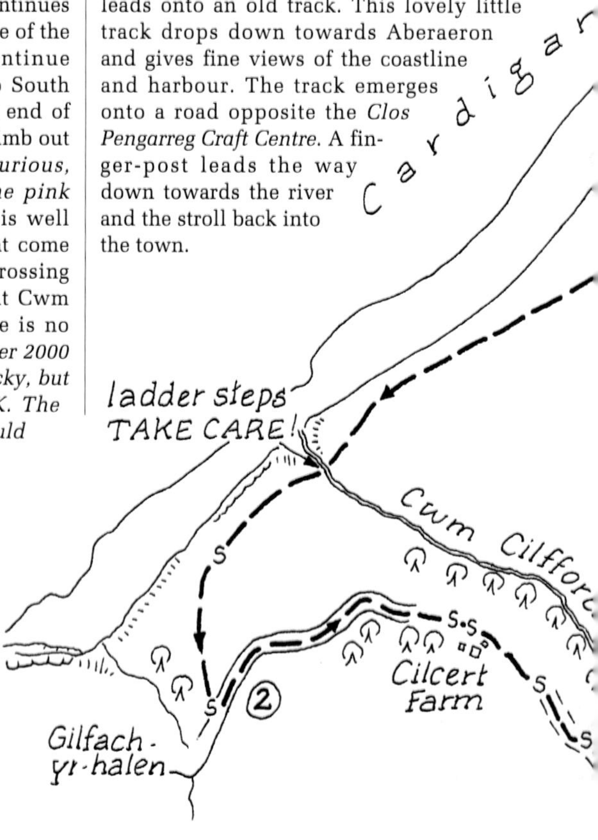

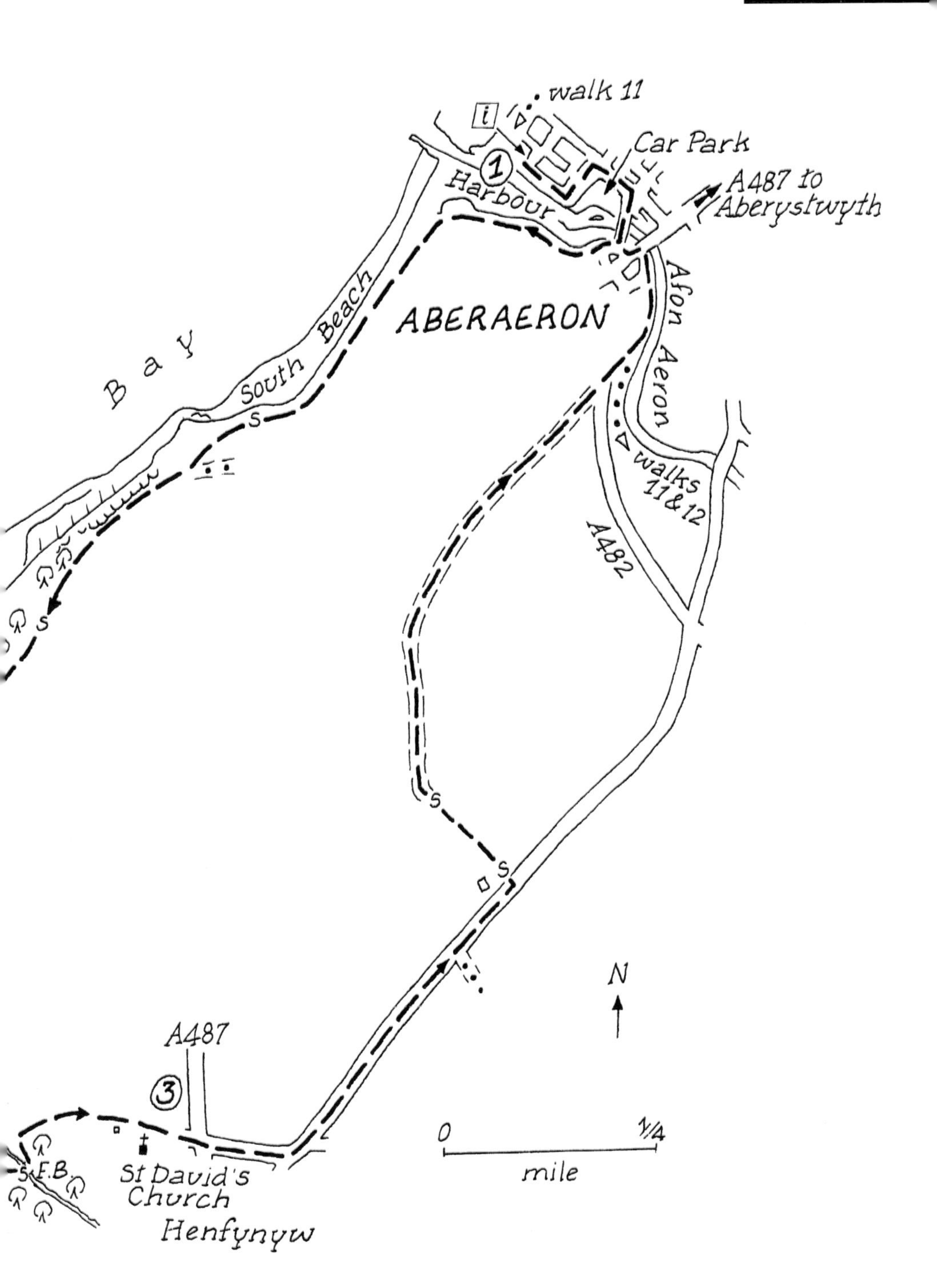
walk 11
i
Car Park
1
Harbour
A487 to
Aberystwyth
Bay
South Beach
ABERAERON
Afon Aeron
S
walks
11&12
A482
S
S
S
N
A487
3
0
1/4
mile
S
F.B.
St David's
Church
Henfynyw

WALK 14
PEN DINAS HILLFORT

DESCRIPTION: This walk to the 415ft summit of Pen Dinas starts from Aberystwyth harbour, which was for many years little more than a creek, with great quantities of herring being landed as early as 1206, making Aberystwyth probably the most important herring port in Wales throughout the Middle Ages. The most significant improvements were made between 1836-1840, with the addition of a southern section, and a replacement of the main wooden jetty with a stone quay. More recently, a marina and modern flats have been added. About 2 – 3 miles.

START: Trefechan bridge at the mouth of the Rheidol river, overlooking Aberystwyth harbour. SN 588812.

In the late 18th century, Aberystwyth was known as 'the Brighton of Wales' with its three hotels – The Talbot; The Gogerddan Arms and The Old Black Lion. By 1807, however, Marine Terrace had been built and the town grew as more accommodation was provided on the sea-front. Today, it's a lively town, with several thousand students swelling the numbers of the local population. It has the biggest Arts Centre in Wales.

1 Go south over Trefechan bridge, passing the Fire Station and the Dinas Terrace turn on the right. Continue along the main road for a few metres more until you reach a finger-post pointing right. This path intersects two fields, and continues up the hill between scrub-covered slopes. The path is well-marked to the summit of the iron-age hillfort of Pen Dinas. *The fort covered the entire hill-top and was home to about 100 Celts. The monument was erected in 1852 to commemorate the Duke of Wellington. It had been the intention to build a statue of the Duke on horseback at the top of the cannon-barrel-shaped monument, but the story goes that the money ran out. From the summit, there are magnificent 360°views of the surrounding countryside and Cardigan Bay.*

2 Pass the monument on your right, and follow the path leading down the hill to where a path from the right joins it. Turn right here and continue down the hill for a few metres before reaching a path T-junction. Turn right and follow this path as it gently makes its way along the side of the hill to the road below. *Looking down, the mile-and-a-half long crescent-shaped beach of shingle and sand the other side of the Ystwyth river is a spectacular sight. This is the best example of a vegetated shingle beach in Ceredigion, and has an area of unusual prostrate blackthorn probably several hundred years old. This hillside and beach are now part of a local nature reserve.*

3 At the bottom of the hill, turn right onto the tarmac road and continue for a few metres to the footpath sign on the left. The path crosses over the site of the former railway line and runs along the back of the former isolation hospital. Turn right onto the tarmac road on the southern edge of the harbour mouth. This road takes you back to the main road and the Fire Station, where you turn left back to Trefechan bridge.

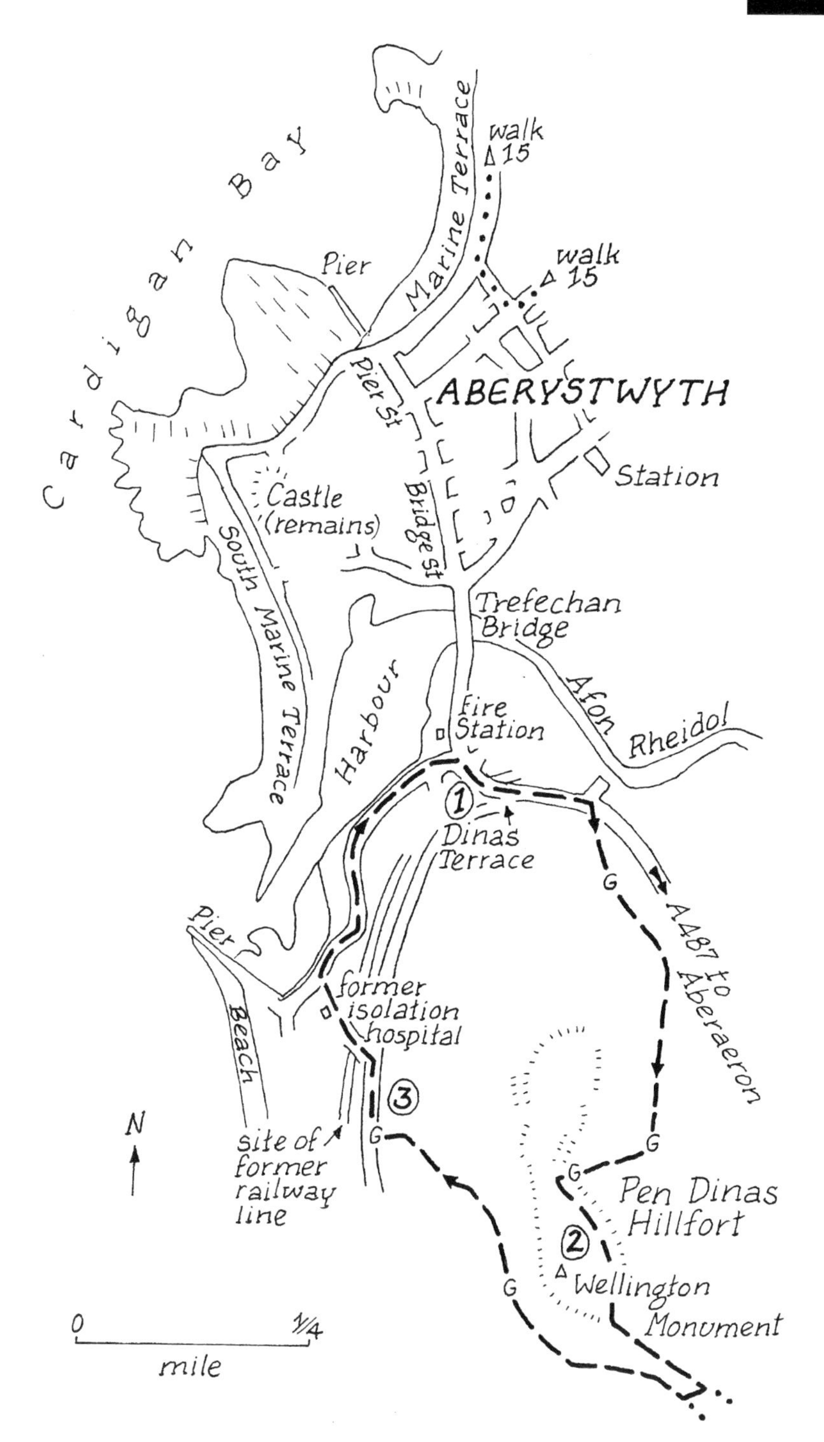
Cardigan Bay
Pier
Marine Terrace
walk 15
walk 15
ABERYSTWYTH
Pier St
Station
Castle (remains)
Bridge St
South Marine Terrace
Trefechan Bridge
Harbour
Afon Rheidol
Fire Station
1
Dinas Terrace
A487 to Aberaeron
Pier
Beach
former isolation hospital
3
G
site of former railway line
N
G
G
Pen Dinas Hillfort
2
Wellington Monument
G
0
1/4
mile

WALK 15

CWM WOODS & PARC NATUR PENGLAIS LOCAL NATURE RESERVE

DESCRIPTION: This is a varied walk combining coastal path, two lovely broad-leaved woodlands and open fields. About 5 miles.
START: Aberystwyth sea-front. SN 587822.

1 From the sea-front head north towards Constitution Hill and its 430 foot summit. For those of you wanting to start this route on a gentle note, the old Cliff Railway, *built in 1896, offers a pleasant alternative to the steep climb that lies ahead. As you ascend by whatever means, you can think back to the Victorians making their way to the top where the 'Lunar Park' with its many attractions awaited them – Constitution Hill at the turn of the 20th century was the focal point for much activity – the café and the largest Camera Obscura in the world still remain, but the bandstand and ballroom have long gone. The millennium beacon now stands as the symbol into the new age. The café and shop are run by a community project which integrates people with learning difficulties into work situations.*

2 The finger-post in front of the café, points you in the direction of Cwm Woods. Follow this track and over a stile to cross fields giving fine views towards Snowdonia and North Wales.

3 The path now enters a conifer woodland where the dark, cool stillness suddenly envelops you. *The densely planted trees, standing tall in regimental rows, allow little light to reach the barren woodland floor.* The path emerges onto a small lane at a U-bend. Carry straight on up the hill, passing two cottages (one derelict) on your right. *In Spring, the pungent smell of ramsons pervades the air.* A footpath sign on the second U-bend leads you straight ahead to enter Cwm Woods. *Unlike the dark conifer plantation, this is a lovely broadleaved woodland full of light and variety.*

4 Continue until you reach a large open old quarried area on your right with glossy ferns growing out of rocky crevices. The path now starts to descend. After about 50 metres the path levels out. Look to your right to see a rough path leading up the bank to the top of the wood. *Half way up, there is a wooden bench made from a tree felled in these woods.* Continue climbing until reaching an old stone wall boundary. Turn right and follow this track to the stile that leads out of the woods.

5 Emerging from the woods, carry on straight ahead across fields *and enjoy the terrific views of the surrounding countryside.* The path is well sign-posted at all the stiles.

6 Where the path joins a track, turn left and follow it down, with the golf course on the right, towards the direction of the sea. *Within the vast sweep of the Bay, Strumble Head, some 50 miles away, and the Presceli mountains, can be seen on a clear day.* Pass by a track that tries to tempt you off to the left and continue down the hill until you reach a small path on the left with a wooden horse barrier set back about 20 metres. Turn left here and follow the path to an old stone stile. Cross this stile and enter the lovely woodland of Parc Natur Penglais. *Massive, dramatic beech trees cast their shade at this spot. It is worth visiting this local nature reserve, particularly in spring as there is a spectacular showing of bluebells – indeed, it is known locally as 'Bluebell Wood'.*

7 Take the track to the right of the beech trees and keep bearing right until you emerge into the strong light of the exposed old quarry. Stone steps on the right lead to the Aberystwyth Panorama Viewpoint. *The interpretation boards here show just how much Aberystwyth developed during the final decade of the last Millennium, with many new buildings springing up along the valley floor.*

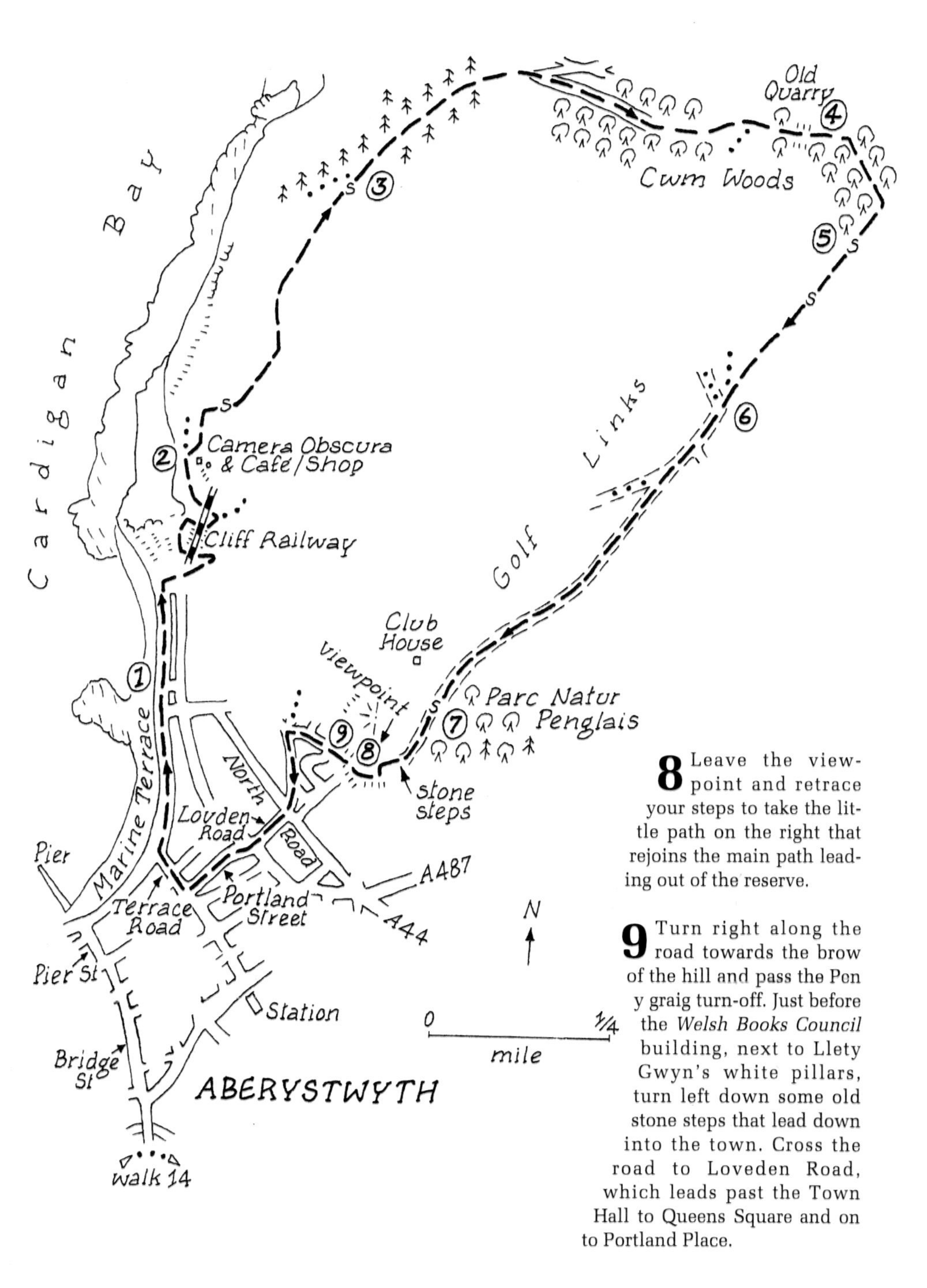

8 Leave the viewpoint and retrace your steps to take the little path on the right that rejoins the main path leading out of the reserve.

9 Turn right along the road towards the brow of the hill and pass the Pen y graig turn-off. Just before the *Welsh Books Council* building, next to Llety Gwyn's white pillars, turn left down some old stone steps that lead down into the town. Cross the road to Loveden Road, which leads past the Town Hall to Queens Square and on to Portland Place.

PRONUNCIATION

These basic points should help non-Welsh speakers

Welsh	**English equivalent**
c	always hard, as in **c**at
ch	as in the Scottish word lo**ch**
dd	as th in **th**en
f	as v in **v**ocal
ff	as **f**
g	always hard as in **g**ot
ll	no real equivalent. It is like 'th' in **th**en, but with an 'L' sound added to it, giving '**thlan**' for the pronunciation of the Welsh 'Llan'.

In Welsh the accent usually falls on the last-but-one syllable of a word.
Llanrhystud – pronounce it 'thlan-rhu-stud' and you will be close!

KEY TO THE MAPS

- Walk route and direction
- Metalled road
- Unsurfaced road
- Fenced track (fence/wall/hedge)
- Footpath/route adjoining walk route
- Railway
- River (afon)/stream (nant) & direction
- Trees
- Shrub/bracken/gorse
- Caravan/chalet park
- G Gate
- S Stile
- F.B. Footbridge
- Marsh
- Viewpoint
- Prominent hilltop (feature)
- P Parking
- T Telephone
- PH Public House
- i Tourist Information Centre

THE COUNTRY CODE

Enjoy the countryside and respect it's life and work
Guard against all risk of fire
Leave gates *as you find them*
Keep your dogs under close control
Keep to public paths across farmland
Use gates and stiles to cross fences, hedges and walls
Leave livestock, crops and machinery alone
Take your litter home
Help to keep all water clean
Protect wildlife, plants and trees
Take special care on country roads
Make no unnecessary noise

Published by
Kittiwake 3 Glantwymyn Village Workshops, Glantwymyn, Machynlleth, Montgomeryshire SY20 8LY

Printed by WPG, Welshpool